FUN AND GAMES

Clockwork Carnival

Measuring Time

Wendy Conklin, M.A.

Consultants

Michele Ogden, Ed.D
Principal, Irvine Unified School District

Jennifer Robertson, M.A.Ed.
Teacher, Huntington Beach City School District

Publishing Credits

Rachelle Cracchiolo, M.S.Ed., *Publisher*
Conni Medina, M.A.Ed., *Managing Editor*
Dona Herweck Rice, *Series Developer*
Emily R. Smith, M.A.Ed., *Series Developer*
Diana Kenney, M.A.Ed., NBCT, *Content Director*
Stacy Monsman, M.A., *Editor*
Kevin Panter, *Graphic Designer*

Image Credits: p. 6 Simon Potter/Getty Images; p.10 incamerastock/Alamy Stock Photo; p. 12 ImagesBazaar/ Getty Images; p. 14 Chicago History Museum/Getty Images; p. 18 Paul Wood/Alamy Stock Photo; p. 20 Dennis MacDonald/Alamy Stock Photo; p. 25 Ann E Parry/ Alamy Stock Photo; all other images from iStock and/or Shutterstock.

Teacher Created Materials

5301 Oceanus Drive
Huntington Beach, CA 92649-1030
http://www.tcmpub.com

ISBN 978-1-4807-5805-6

Table of Contents

Getting Ready for the Carnival

"Wake up, sleepyhead! Aren't we going to the **carnival** today?" These words wake you from a deep sleep. Every year, you wait for the carnival. You think about the fun rides. You dream about the special food. And don't forget the magic show and petting zoo! It seems as though this day has taken forever to arrive, and now it's finally here!

You jump out of bed and look at the **clock**. It is already 10:15 a.m. It will take you 15 **minutes** to eat, 5 minutes to get dressed, and 2 minutes to brush your teeth. What **time** will you be ready to go to the carnival?

candy apples

It's now 10:37 a.m. You are almost out the door when you're reminded of your chores. Your dog, Zeus, won't get walked if you don't do it. So, you grab the leash and take him outside. When you get back, it's 11:10 a.m.

Now, where's that carnival ticket? The search begins in your messy room. Is it under the bed or in your drawers? After 12 minutes of searching, you find it in your pocket.

Your family could walk to the carnival, but that would take 45 minutes. And it might make you tired. Luckily, the bus comes by every 15 minutes. You get to the bus stop at 11:30 a.m. The next bus comes by in 10 minutes. So, you wait for it. The ride takes 25 minutes. What time do you get to the carnival?

LET'S EXPLORE MATH

1. How many minutes does it take to walk Zeus? How do you know?

2. If you walk to the carnival, what time will you get there? How do you know?

3. How many minutes do you save by taking the bus instead of walking?

Time for Fun!

Finally, you arrive at the carnival with your family. You see the bumper cars and the carousel nearby. Each ride lasts five minutes. Which one will you ride first?

The line for the bumper cars is long, but it's your favorite ride. You like how the cars bump against one another and get trapped in the corner. The sign says it will be a 30-minute wait. But no one is in line for the carousel. You decide to start with the carousel and then get in line to wait for the bumper cars. How many minutes does it take for you to ride both rides?

log flume

10

Finding Funnel Cakes

The log **flume** is so close. After a brisk 5-minute walk, you decide to take a ride to cool off. At the top of the log flume's highest hill, you get a **bird's-eye view** of the carnival. You can see the Ferris wheel in the distance. After 12 minutes of watery fun, you decide to ride it next.

But as you walk to the Ferris wheel, the smell of **funnel cake** fills the air. It gets stronger during your 8-minute walk. Your stomach grumbles. Instead of following the crowd to the Ferris wheel, you follow your nose to the food stand that is close by. For 5 sweet minutes, you enjoy every bite. How many minutes does it take you to get soaked, walk, and eat your snack?

strawberry funnel cake

11

At the Magic Show

It's 1:15 p.m. With a stomach full of funnel cake, going on a ride that spins in circles might not be the best idea. You don't want to feel sick at the carnival. That would ruin your whole day! What activity might let you rest for a bit, but still have fun? You see that a magic show will begin at 1:30 p.m. The theater is right around the corner. Luckily, a seat in the front row is waiting for you.

The show begins four minutes late, but it is worth the wait. The **magician** pulls a rabbit out of an empty hat. He saws his assistant into two pieces. Then, he pulls a goldfish out of someone's ear. Finally, he crawls into a box and disappears. All of this takes 30 minutes. By the time it is over, your stomach feels fine. Now, back to those rides!

The Fabulous Ferris Wheel

Your watch says 2:04 p.m. The Ferris wheel pauses to load new people. You wait in line for five minutes and step on board. There are not many riders. It only takes another six minutes for the rest of the people to board.

As you wait, you read a sign. It has information about the very first Ferris wheel. People rode the first Ferris wheel in 1893. One turn around took 20 minutes!

Finally, the wait is over, and the Ferris wheel goes round and round. From the top, you can see the entire carnival. After just nine minutes, your ride is over. It is your turn to step off the Ferris wheel. That was so much fun!

The first Ferris wheel debuted at the 1893 Chicago World's Fair.

1. Use the clocks to find out how many minutes it takes to wait for, load, and ride the Ferris wheel.

2. How much longer was the ride time in 1893 compared to the ride time today? How do you know?

3. How does pausing to load and unload riders affect the time it takes to ride the Ferris wheel?

15

Waiting Instead of Riding

By the time you walk to the next ride, it is 2:30 p.m. The line for the **pendulum** ride winds around it twice! You have a bit of a wait ahead of you, but you know it will be worth it. From the ground, the pendulum swings from one side to the other. You feel a tickle in your stomach as you watch it swing. Happy riders scream with excitement. This is going to be fun! After 10 minutes, you get closer to the front of the line.

When you finally get there, the worker puts up a sign— "Closed for **maintenance**." You don't want to give up your place in line, so you wait. Much to your dismay, the ride takes 45 minutes to reopen, but at least you get your turn.

1. Use the **number line** to figure out how long you wait for the pendulum ride.

2. What time is it when you are finished waiting?

3. The ride was fun, but was it worth it to wait? Why or why not? Instead of waiting in line, what else could you have done?

10 minutes   45 minutes

2:30 2:35 2:40 2:45 2:50 2:55 3:00 3:05 3:10 3:15 3:20 3:25

Extending the Fun

Your watch tells you that it is 3:25 p.m. You walk to the games area and see the basketball hoops. You also see people trying to toss small balls into fishbowls. And then there's the ringtoss game. Which one should you play? Tossing rings looks like fun, but you really want to win the prize at the basketball game. It turns out the choice isn't as tough as you thought.

The basketball game only takes 2 minutes. You walk away a winner! But, the stuffed animal is way too big to carry. So you look for a locker to keep it safe. After 30 minutes, you find a locker. You put the stuffed animal inside. What time is it now?

3:25

Dinnertime

At 4:00 p.m., you arrive at the food stands. You need a meal to eat, not just a snack. One stand is selling corn dogs. Another stand has roasted turkey legs. You also see hamburgers and fries. What do you want to eat? It will take 2 minutes to get a corn dog. The turkey leg stand has a 10-minute wait. The wait for a hamburger and fries is 5 minutes. You know that you want to spend as much time as you can at the petting zoo before it closes. So, you check a map and see that it will take you 5 minutes to walk there. The map also tells you that the petting zoo closes at 4:30 p.m. You have a big decision to make.

Food	Wait Time	Time It Takes to Eat
corn dog	2 minutes	8 minutes
turkey leg	10 minutes	8 minutes
hamburger and fries	5 minutes	8 minutes

1. It takes you 5 minutes to walk to the petting zoo. When will you get to the petting zoo if you order and eat the corn dog? The turkey leg? The hamburger and fries?

2. Which food line will allow you the most time at the petting zoo? How many minutes will you have there?

3. Which food choice will allow you the least time at the petting zoo? How many minutes will you have there?

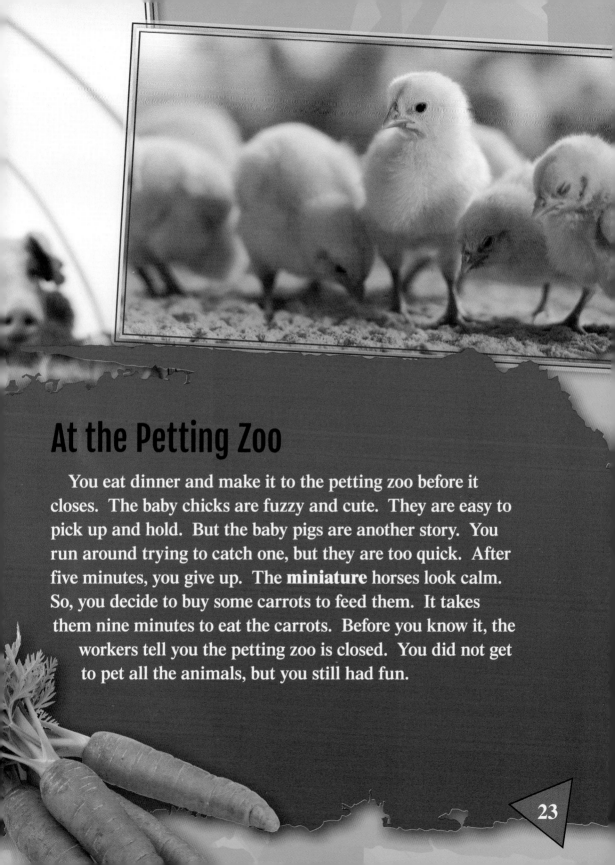

At the Petting Zoo

You eat dinner and make it to the petting zoo before it closes. The baby chicks are fuzzy and cute. They are easy to pick up and hold. But the baby pigs are another story. You run around trying to catch one, but they are too quick. After five minutes, you give up. The **miniature** horses look calm. So, you decide to buy some carrots to feed them. It takes them nine minutes to eat the carrots. Before you know it, the workers tell you the petting zoo is closed. You did not get to pet all the animals, but you still had fun.

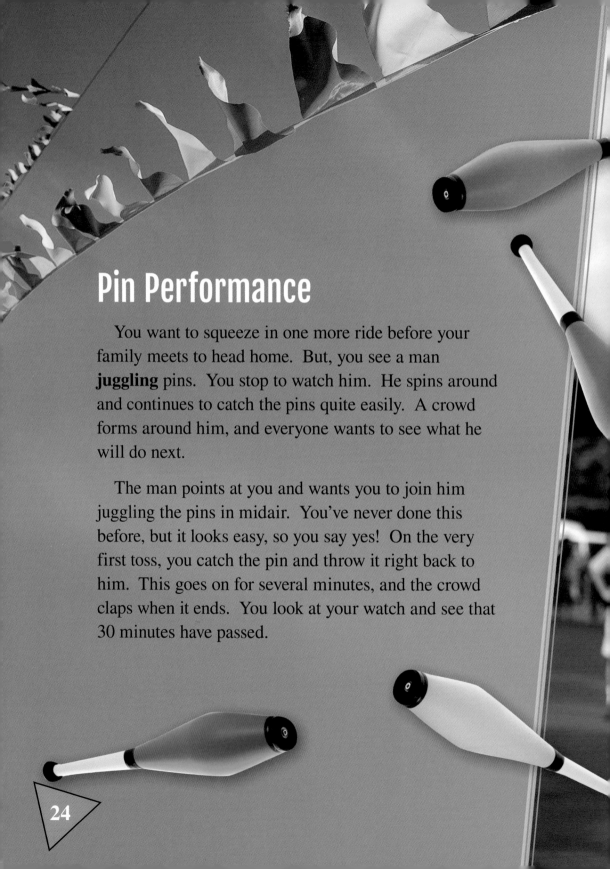

Pin Performance

You want to squeeze in one more ride before your family meets to head home. But, you see a man **juggling** pins. You stop to watch him. He spins around and continues to catch the pins quite easily. A crowd forms around him, and everyone wants to see what he will do next.

The man points at you and wants you to join him juggling the pins in midair. You've never done this before, but it looks easy, so you say yes! On the very first toss, you catch the pin and throw it right back to him. This goes on for several minutes, and the crowd claps when it ends. You look at your watch and see that 30 minutes have passed.

A Day of Good Times

Before you know it, it's 5:00 p.m. The next bus arrives in 30 minutes. The swing around ride is near the front gate of the carnival. So, you to ride it before heading back to bus stop. The wait and the ride only take 15 minutes. Then, you go to the locker to get your stuffed animal. You make your way out of the carnival and to the bus stop. That takes another 12 minutes.

You think about all the fun you had during the day as you get on the bus with your family. What was the best part of the day? Was it the food, the show, the rides, the petting zoo, or the games? You can't decide because you liked it all and can't wait to come back next year!

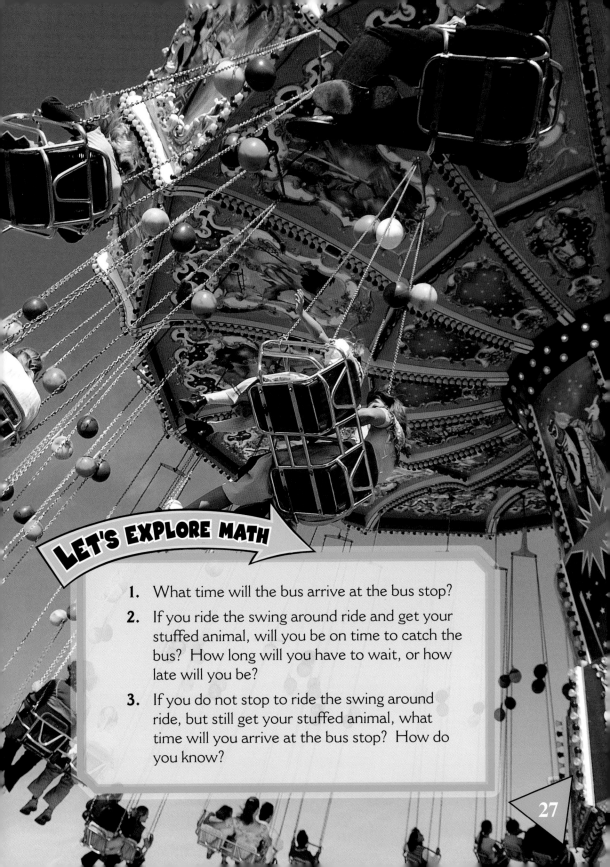

1. What time will the bus arrive at the bus stop?

2. If you ride the swing around ride and get your stuffed animal, will you be on time to catch the bus? How long will you have to wait, or how late will you be?

3. If you do not stop to ride the swing around ride, but still get your stuffed animal, what time will you arrive at the bus stop? How do you know?

⚙️ Problem Solving

It's the end of the day and almost time to go home from the carnival. Miguel wants to ride more rides, but he only has 35 minutes remaining. Answer the questions to find out how Miguel plans his time.

1. Which two rides will take the most amount of time? How do you know?

2. Which ride will take the least amount of time? How do you know?

3. Design a plan for Miguel so that he can ride as many rides as possible in 35 minutes.

Ride	Wait Time	Ride Time
Octopus	8 minutes	4 minutes
Tilt-a-Whirl	3 minutes	3 minutes
Arctic Plunge	6 minutes	8 minutes
Tornado	10 minutes	3 minutes
Loop-O-Plane	9 minutes	7 minutes

Glossary

bird's-eye-view—a view from a high place, as if seen from a bird's perspective

carnival—a traveling amusement park with rides, games, food, and shows

clock—a tool that shows time

flume—a sloping channel for carrying water

funnel cake—deep-fried batter sprinkled with powdered sugar

juggling—keeping several objects in the air by throwing and catching them

magician—a person who does tricks that seem impossible

maintenance—act of making repairs or fixing problems so that equipment stays working and safe

miniature—very small

minutes—units of time that are 60 seconds long

number line—math picture and problem solving tool with numbers at certain points on a straight line

pendulum—something that has weight on the bottom so that it swings back and forth

time—the attribute that is measured in minutes, seconds, hours, days, and years

Index

Answer Key

Let's Explore Math

page 7:

1. 33 min.; 10:37 to 11:00 is 23 min., plus 10 more min. is 11:10 a.m.

2. 12:07 p.m.; 11:10 plus 12 min. to find the ticket is 11:22 a.m. 11:22 to 12:00 is 38 min. I still need 7 more min., so 12:00 plus 7 min. is 12:07 p.m.

3. 10 min.; 45 − 10 − 25 = 10

page 15:

1. 20 min.

2. 11 min. longer; 20 − 9 = 11, or 9 + 11 = 20

3. It takes longer to board more people, so the Ferris wheel ride takes longer.

page 17:

1. 55 min.

2. 3:25 p.m.

3. Answers will vary, but may include: The ride wasn't worth the wait because I could have ridden other rides or played games instead of waiting.

page 21:

1. 4:15 p.m., 4:23 p.m., 4:18 p.m.

2. corn dog line; 15 min.

3. turkey leg line; 7 min.

page 27:

1. 5:30 p.m.

2. Yes; wait 3 min.

3. 5:12 p.m.; it takes 12 min. to get the stuffed animal, and 5:00 plus 12 min. is 5:12 p.m.

Problem Solving

1. Arctic Plunge and the Loop-O-Plane; will take 14 min. and 16 min., and no other rides have greater totals

2. Tilt-a-Whirl; will take 6 min., and it is the least amount of time

3. Octopus, Tilt-a-Whirl, and Tornado; will take 31 min. (12 + 6 + 13 = 31). By picking the rides with the least total min., Miguel gets to go on 3 rides.